# Finch Foundry

Devon

**National Trust**

*FORGE OR FOUNDRY?*
'Finch Foundry' is a misnomer. It is in fact a forge: it has forges and furnaces where metals are heated prior to shaping (*wrought*). It is doubtful that it was ever used as a foundry, to *cast* metal, but the name has stuck – perhaps because the first Finch to move here, William, worked at one of the many iron foundries nearby before coming to Sticklepath.

*Above* The leat in Sticklepath

*Right* One of the water-wheels at the foundry

# THE VILLAGE OF MILLS

The River Taw runs through the village of Sticklepath on the northern edge of Dartmoor. Gushing down a steep valley known as Belstone Cleave, it supplies the power that once made this the 'village of mills'. In the 19th century there would have been as many as four watermills and seven water-wheels in the village. Today, only one mill survives: Finch Foundry.

## One site, many mills

There have been mills where Finch Foundry stands for over 700 years. They have been used to produce food, cloth and finally agricultural tools, reflecting fickle markets, advancing technology and the changing needs of the villagers. Alongside agriculture and mining, mills would have played an important part in village life here, providing a livelihood for many villagers.

In medieval times the grist mill and fulling mill on the site belonged to the Manor of Sampford Courtenay. The grist mill ground corn into flour for the manor. Next door, the fulling mill was used to treat cloth to make it suitable for use, so that it could then go to a woollen mill and become *serge*, a coarse material for which the area was famous. In the 18th century the fulling mill became a woollen mill.

The leat, a man-made watercourse at the rear of the foundry, channels water away from the river to the mills to power the water-wheels before discharging back into the river at the western end of the village.

## The mill as we know it

The story of Finch Foundry begins in 1814. By that time the woollen mill had closed, following the collapse of the Devon woollen industry. Under the management of the Finch family, the woollen mill became the forge, and the grist mill a grinding house. This is when Finch Foundry came into its own, gaining its reputation for producing high-quality 'edge-tools', designed for cutting.

It remained the site of the family business until 1960, when lack of maintenance and the heavy vibrations generated by the forge's trip hammers caused the rear wall to collapse. The foundry was restored as a working museum, saved by Richard Barron and a team of volunteers, and was given to the National Trust in 1994 by the North Dartmoor Museums Association, made possible by a bequest from Mr W.A. Espley.

Once a common sight, a foundry of this type is now rare working proof of our industrial past. Although it no longer produces the 400 tools daily that it did in its heyday, the three water-wheels still drive the hammers, grindstones and other machinery, demonstrating how tools were made when water was the key source of industrial power.

*Origins of a name*
The village is named after the sharply raised ridge or path on which it stands ('staecle' is the Anglo-Saxon word for steep).

*Top* Sticklepath in the 19th century

*Above* The village post office

3

Finch Foundry was set up in 1814, when William Finch leased the former woollen factory. During his time, nine members of the Finch family worked for the firm. Six or seven open blacksmith's hearths and anvils, and two roaring furnaces would have been enclosed in the single building. As the business grew in the 1850s, the family leased the old grist mill building and installed a grindstone, which allowed them to expand their range of products.

*Above* Rebecca Finch and her three sons (*from left*) James, Thomas Seacombe and Albany George, with their families around 1890. Rebecca Finch was a Victorian matriarch dedicated to the wellbeing of the foundry and its workers. She worked alongside her husband George until he died from a laudanum overdose (taken to combat toothache) in 1885, forcing her to assume full control. As well as being concerned with the central business of the foundry, she also ran a shop and post office from the front room of Foundry House, next to the forge, to help bring in extra money

## Finding a niche

Finch Foundry was not just a workshop producing edge-tools. Having acquired both mills, the Finches roofed over the area between to give them more space for a saw mill, as well as carpenters' and wheelwrights' shops. The foundry could then produce handles for its tools and make carts, wagons, gates, hurdles and even coffins.

The Finches proved to be successful entrepreneurs, meeting the needs of specialist markets. They also made ship and boat parts: one expertise was the provision of selected timber for 'boat knees' (naturally curved timbers that were used in boat construction), which went to the shipyards in Plymouth. Since so much coal was used to fuel the forge, the Finches also became coal merchants.

## A line of Finches

Born in the nearby village of Spreyton in 1779, William Finch lived and worked as a blacksmith in Tavistock before deciding to branch out and set up Finch Foundry with his second wife, Susannah. The trade stayed with the Finch family – the 1851 census for Sticklepath lists William Finch and five of his sons as edge-tool makers. Generally, management passed down the male line, but women did get involved: Emlin Finch ran the business from 1873 until 1882, and a few years later Rebecca Finch took charge. The last Finch to run the foundry was Ralph Finch from 1945 to 1960, along with Richard Barron and Charles Bowden, both related.

### Hard times

Times were tough in the second half of the 19th century, as industrialisation in the Midlands and north of England threatened many traditional Devon crafts, and cheap imports from British colonies provided stiff competition. In the 1830s the Crediton and Okehampton workhouses were set up after the decline of the Devon woollen industry. The Finch family business survived for longer than most other edge-tool manufacturers in the area.

### Service to schoolchildren

An unusual role that the foundry played was to dry out wet children. In the 19th century, children were often soaked when it rained during their walk of up to three miles to school. The headteacher would send them to Finch Foundry with a note saying, 'Dear Mr Finch, please dry out these children'.

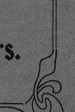

*Above* The versatility of materials used by the Finches is demonstrated by products such as these wooden scythe handles

*Left* Cover of the Finch Brothers catalogue

All the tools were made in batches according to seasonal demand: hay knives and heavy hedging tools in autumn and winter, and bramble hooks and hoes in spring and summer. To make best use of materials, small items like the potato chopper were made with the metal off-cuts from the production of larger tools.

Materials were not limited to the West Country. The Finch brothers firm also sold hickory axe and pick handles imported from the US via a firm in Bristol, and finished off steel-faced shovel plates from Belbroughton, Worcestershire.

Producing iron edge-tools by hand was highly specialised work. The Finches made fifteen types of hook and six differently shaped shovels, as well as tools for the agricultural, mining and china clay industries.

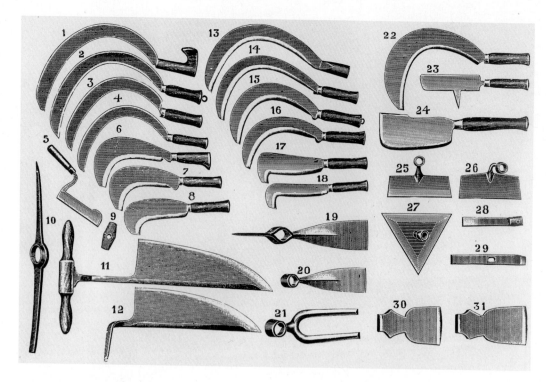

*Above* The range of edge-tools on offer

## The Finch repertoire

The range of edge-tools produced was staggering, including reap hooks, crank grass hooks, straight grass hooks, Devon potato choppers, bramble hooks, Cornish furze hooks, swan-neck hooks, weed irons, turf irons, winged turf irons, twibills, mattocks, Kent axes, Cornish and Devon shovels. These were crafted on site, even down to the straw-rope packaging, which was made at the rear of Foundry House.

## Wondrous wood

Aside from iron, raw materials used at the foundry included wood, felled locally. Sawn ash was made into cart shafts, wheel felloes (rims) and tool handles; elm was used for wheel naves (hubs) and coffin boards; oak

for wheel spokes; holly for the heads of beetles or mauls (large mallets for driving fence posts); and larch for gates and hurdles.

## Selling Finch products in all the land

Although sold throughout the West Country, Finch tools were best known in Devon and were synonymous with high-quality iron products. In the late 19th century, carts piled high with tools would make the long trek to markets or country fairs as far away as Taunton, Bridport and Penzance.

Albany George Finch acted as a travelling salesman for the firm at this time – his notebook records a 'Cornwall journey' which consisted of two separate journeys of about a week each. He visited 40 towns and villages and 170 customers, including mine owners, china clay producers, foundries, agricultural merchants and even saddlers. In 1822, when no cart was available, a heavily pregnant Susannah Finch, wife of William, apparently walked the 20 miles to Tavistock fair laden with bill-hooks. She returned having sold them all *and* given birth to her daughter, Mary.

*What made a good-quality tool?*
Although some cutting tools had hardened edges, these were expensive and required a great deal of skill to produce. As a result, everyday tools were made from cheaper wrought iron, which is relatively soft and would wear away quickly.

The Finch brothers produced hard-wearing tools, applying a standard technique used in the production of Samurai swords. The tools were made of a sandwich of two bars of wrought iron around a bar of 'blister steel' (an early form of hardened steel). All three bars were fixed together and placed in a furnace, heated to about 1300° Fahrenheit (704° Celsius) and hammered rapidly to forge-weld them into one bar. This bar was then reheated and forged into whatever tool was required. Finally, the metal was ground on the large grindstone, exposing the hard steel along the cutting edge.

*Above* The many varieties of hay forks sold

*Above left* The Custodian of Finch Foundry demonstrates how tools are heated in the furnace

*Left* A receipt dated Christmas 1936

## THE FOUNDRY IN ACTION

1   Water-wheels

2   Belts and wheels

3   Drop hammers

There are two drop hammers at Finch today. The larger one weighs 82kg (as heavy as a tall man). The smaller one is used for little tools, and the larger one for shaping shovel blades.

4   Trip hammers

The trip hammer marks progress towards mass production, enabling a line of almost identical tools to be made. Finch Foundry is the only water-powered forge in England where a working trip hammer can be seen.

The foundry has two trip hammers. The largest, at 1171kg, was known as the 'plating hammer' and, as the name suggests, was used to hammer out the plate required for shovel blades. The smaller 'steeling hammer' weighs 726kg and strikes 240 beats per minute. This was used to forge-weld together the wrought iron and blister steel used in tool manufacture.

The strike rate was important, as at that speed the hammer actually generates heat. This heat helps to maintain the temperature of the metal, crucial in achieving a 'forge weld'. The vibrations from these hammers were so severe that the local pub had to have a rim fitted to the shelf above the bar to stop their glasses bouncing off it.

5   Shears

To operate the shears, the strap at the end of the lever arm is attached to the drive wheel as it turned round. The steel blades on the shears were used to cut red hot bars of metal up to 13mm thick. Smaller shears were used to trim the shovel blades to shape. The shears would have been used primarily at the start of the day to provide sufficient cut material for the day's production.

6   Furnaces

Originally, there were six forges and two furnaces in the foundry, each having a specific use. All are located close to where the heated metal would be worked.

The forges were used to provide a more localised heat for shaping the various tools, whilst the furnaces would provide a large amount of heat over a wide area. They would have heated the plate for spade blades, prior to shaping under the drop hammers. The larger furnace would have heated several bundles of metal before they were forge-welded under the steeling hammer.

## Overshot or undershot?

**Overshot wheels**, such as the ones at Finch Foundry, are turned by water falling into the wheel's buckets from above. They are often found in hilly areas on rivers with a consistent flow

**Undershot wheels**, where the water powers the wheel from below, hitting the blades at a low level, require rivers with a large volume of fast-flowing water and are less efficient than overshot wheels

# TOUR OF THE FOUNDRY

The metal-working machinery at Finch Foundry today is now unique, recording the beginnings of the mechanisation of the edge-tool industry. Parts of it are over 200 years old. What you see today gives a good impression of the foundry as it would have been in the 19th century.

## Water-wheels

The three overshot water-wheels are the key to the foundry's power. They convert the energy of the fast-flowing water into mechanical power. Each wheel has a distinct role:

- One wheel drives the grindstone, the polishing wheel and the bandsaw for cutting wood
- Another drives the trip hammers, the drop hammers and the shears
- The third drives the fan that blasts air through underground ducts to the furnaces and forges

### Transferring power

Electrical energy can flow through cables of any length. In contrast, power from the wheels is transmitted mechanically by means of shafts, pulleys, belts, cogs and gear wheels that lead directly from the wheel to the tool or grindstone. This means that each tool (fan, grindstone, hammer or shears) has to be situated close to the water-wheel to keep shafts as short as possible – which is both safer and more economical.

### Renewable energy

Water power is a sustainable alternative to energy produced from fossil fuels – it does not emit any of the noxious or greenhouse gases associated with fossil-fuelled power plants, such as carbon dioxide. The wheels used to harness energy at Finch are the precursor to sophisticated electricity-generating turbines, which also use water as a renewable energy source.

### A fatal power

The axle of the forge water-wheel at the foundry and the wheels it carries weigh about seven tons – an impressive but dangerous force. A member of the family died under the smaller fan wheel when it was going at full pelt in 1849. Edwin Finch, the five-year-old son of Joseph Finch, was playing near a water-wheel when his toy became trapped in it. Edwin was dragged under the wheel. His physically disabled brother was nearby but could not help. Their cries were not heard over the foundry noises, and Edwin drowned.

*Above* The shafts, pulleys and gear wheels that transfer the power generated by the water-wheel to the foundry machinery. The water-powered shears are on the right with the anvil in the background

*Left* One of the water-wheels in the 19th century

*Opposite* The water-wheel turning today

11

The trip hammer drops, pulleys turn, metal clashes and sparks fly. With its uneven earthen floor and towering, ear-splitting machinery, not to mention the fiercely hot furnace, this building is the hub of the works, beating out the rhythmical thudding noise of the hammer that echoes around the village, signalling that the foundry is in action.

### What happens here?
Metal is heated and beaten into shape. See pages 8 and 9 for an explanation of the drop hammers, trip hammers, shears and furnaces.

### Grinding shop
The grindstone was used to sharpen the tools produced in the forge. The wheel that powered the grindstone also drove a band saw, which cut the curved sections of timber used in wheel and wagon building, and a polishing wheel.

The grindstone ran in a trough of water, which kept it lubricated and prevented the metal overheating and losing its 'temper' (hardness). The grinder was located face down above the stone, away from splashes.

The grinder would operate the grindstone with his left hand, pulling a lever that struck the belt from the overhead pulley on to a fast pulley. The same hand would also pull the lever that controlled the *penstock*, the sluice that governed the amount of water delivered to the wheel and therefore affected the speed and power of the turning stone.

### Did you know?
A new grindstone was 165cm wide and 20cm thick, and within six months it could be worn away to half its size. It is easy to see why the expression 'nose to the grindstone' came about.

A grinder's work was unpleasant. Working at the polishing wheel, however, had its perks – men could earn a treat such as a pint of cider by polishing the bottoms of flat irons belonging to women in the village.

*Below* The pulley mechanism in action in the grinding house

*Top* Metal being heated in
the forge

*Above* Cutting hot metal
with the shears

*Left* Sharpening a sickle
with the grindstone

13

## LEARNING THE TRADE

Often apprentices were recruited by word of mouth, and it was considered an honour to be taken on. Walter Bradford was apprenticed at the age of fourteen by George Finch as a 'learner in Wheelwrighting/Undertaking' and was commended for 'Regularity and punctuality'. Trade apprenticeships could last from five to seven years. Once finished, the worker became a 'journeyman' and was expected to learn from others elsewhere, before returning to his original employers to repay them for his training. In practice, though, many workers never honoured this.

*Right* The trip hammer, once used by John Mallet

The average working day was long, often starting at 6am. Since the Finches built and repaired farm wagons and shoed horses, working hours were dictated by the farmers. They required a dawn-till-dusk service six days a week, Sunday being a day of prayer and rest.

### A craftsman's career

The workforce had its own hierarchy, with the youngest 'boy' at the bottom. The learning process was often harsh, with beatings for mistakes common. The apprentice's day was the longest, beginning with lighting the forges and furnaces ready for the day ahead, and not finishing until the foundry had been tidied and fires laid for the following day.

The ultimate goal was to become a craftsman, since one's skill and ability often dictated social standing within the community. The workforce would act as a family, proud of the workplace and their joint ability.

At the top of the tree was the aptly named John Mallet (standing on the left of the group in the photograph), who had reached the dizzy heights of 'Hammer Man'. He had the skill to use the trip hammers – the whole business relied on him.

### Work for all

For six days a week the foundry would have been a hive of industry, with people, wagons and horses coming and going all day. If work became scarce, the workers were often employed on the land owned by the Finch family, particularly at harvest time. It is hard to imagine the heat, smoke, smell and noise of the foundry, when a workforce of 20–25 were shoeing horses, making carts and producing hundreds of tools per day.

### Community spirit

Despite the hard working conditions, the foundry was probably warmer and drier than the cottages in which many of the men lived. Their camaraderie and pride in their work blunted much of the discomfort and hardship. The foundry would also have been the social focus of the community, a place to meet and exchange gossip. Many people in the area lived in scattered communities and worked long hours – they would rarely have had the opportunity to stop and chat.

*Above* The schedule of workers at Finch was dictated by the needs of agricultural workers such as these at Arlington Court in Devon

*Left* Workers at Finch Foundry around 1900. George Albany Finch is in the middle row, second from left. Each worker would have developed a particular skill: this and the speed at which they could work was crucial in making the production of 400 tools per day possible. You can tell each man's skill from the tool he holds. Among them are blacksmiths, carpenters, the hammer man (who operated the trip hammer), a wheelwright and a farrier

### The Garden
In the Finches' time the garden would have been divided into allotments and used to grow vegetables. These allotments had evolved from the medieval burgage plots that can still be seen to the north of Sticklepath. The planting and design of this garden developed from the 1950s, largely created by Joyce and Richard Barron just before Finch Foundry became a museum.

### Protecting Finch Foundry
The machinery and tools at the foundry are some of the last of their kind, and the site itself is statutorily protected. A great deal of work goes on behind the scenes to ensure that Finch Foundry survives to tell its story.

Since the Trust took over, we have carried out major renovations, such as restoring the main water-wheel that runs the trip hammers. As you can imagine, the water that surrounds and powers the foundry is not good for the metal machinery, and great care has to be taken to clean and protect every piece of metal to prevent it from rusting. If a piece of machinery needs repairing, archaeologists are often brought in to oversee any changes, and new parts have to be individually made by a specialist.

Every day, the custodian checks all the machinery and tools to confirm that they are safe, and then the last working water-powered forge in the south of England is opened for all to see.

*Top* The garden today

*Above* Foundry products

*Right* Preparing a new water wheel shaft at Finch Foundry